TOSKA

Alina Pleskova's debut collection is into grabbing things by the neck, & not always gently: eros in the ancient bedroom & the age of apps; transcendence & complacency & spirituality under capitalism. Pleskova's poetics is deliciously generous, even in its moments of ambivalence; reading *Toska* is like chatting with your best friend about pursuing & evading pleasure while the American project unravels. These poems don't just see to the heart of queer & immigrant subjectivities; they enact them. I sank with this book, was buoyed by this book—how it, like so many of us in America, experiences perpetual attempt, failed translation, the feeling that we are always missing something just beyond our reach. If only we could tighten our grip, want wanting itself, we might unearth language for identity & desire— language, of course, being ephemeral, timeless, fleeting, & stunning, all at once.

—RAENA SHIRALI, author of *summonings* and *GILT*

These are poems about the untranslatable but essential concepts that form us, and Alina Pleskova is the interpreter of their simultaneous hold and flight: "What you call me in the dark / isn't what I am / & that helps me float / above the moment." *Toska* is a book of the immigrant daughter in her not-quite-own world, and a book of contempt for striving and capitalism—but the centripetal force that powers these poems is the nameless part of the self, "ruthlessly / down for whatever," the locked room that nobody can open even while you long for a breach. Pleskova, generous and funny and modern, is a poet of forthright intimacy.

—NIINA POLLARI, author of *Path of Totality*

Reading *Toska* was a spiritual and whole-body experience. I laughed, I screamed, I teared up, I nearly bought a one-way ticket back to Moldova, I called my mom. No one captures the poetics of eros and diasporic longing amid our late-stage capitalist hellscape like Alina Pleskova. "Assuring various robots / that I'm not a robot several times daily" does not prevent our speaker from "stockpil[ing] intimacies almost too ephemeral to clock." And what a gift this book of intimacies is. *Toska* is a tender and wry instruction manual for navigating desire and the void. I will follow Alina Pleskova anywhere.

—RUTH MADIEVSKY, author of *All-Night Pharmacy*

Alina Pleskova's *Toska* bears the burden of the eponymous longing melancholy of living even as it phases into the burn of real threats to human—and humane—existence. Writing from "The country where I live— / its surveillance of us surveilled by the country I'm from—" she counterpoints the impersonal gaze of the state and algorithms that follow our movements with the poet's infinitely careful attention to the flow of the everyday: "Made it this far / without mentioning the rain. // Here it is; it's perfect." Solace is found in community, the imperative to "Daydream what mutual care could do," the vast motions astrology tracks, ancient poet gossip. Overwhelmingly, too, in the mysteries of queer desire and its dream of transcendence, the desire to desire unbounded by intolerance, or worse—murder. These poems telegraph in a seductive whisper that keeping each other alive is enough—it's everything, because "I want the class wars to start, but everyone's so tired." The poet asks, "What song was playing when my heart's chambers / got thrown open to let these breezes in?" This book is the song, its frequencies coming through the voices of friends, lovers, family, the poets of the past, and Pleskova's tender plaint that would "Mourn the redwoods, fireflies, platypuses, permafrost, all else that deserves to outlive us & won't . . ." In her hands, poetry is the hack for our earthly hangover, *toska / saudade* its secret sauce in whose ingredients hide the seeds of a new world. We'll be together there, "covered in each other's hair."

—ANA BOŽIČEVIĆ, author of *New Life*

TOSKA

TOSKA

Poems

Alina Pleskova

DEEP VELLUM PUBLISHING
DALLAS, TEXAS

Deep Vellum Publishing
3000 Commerce St., Dallas,Texas 75226
deepvellum.org · @deepvellum

Deep Vellum is a 501c3 nonprofit literary arts organization
founded in 2013 with the mission to bring
the world into conversation through literature.

ISBNs: 9781646052721 (paperback) | 9781646052936 (eBook)

Library Of Congress Control Number: 2023005414

Support for this publication has been provided in part by the National Endowment for the Arts, the
Texas Commission on the Arts, the City of Dallas Office of Arts and Culture, and the George and Fay
Young Foundation

Cover artist: Katy Horan
Typesetting by www.INeedABookInterior.com

Printed in the United States of America

"Meanwhile the story of your life becomes the story of
the detours your desire takes"

LAUREN BERLANT, *Desire/Love*

"There's a dialogue I tumble into during orgasm, it goes /
What do you know about people's souls? / Hardly anything"

CHRISTOPHER NEALON, *The Shore*

TABLE OF CONTENTS

TAKE CARE

I've been trying to remember where I am.
On the phone I said

this feeling is so familiar, like a long
drive & no recollection of steering.

There's never an arrival point—only
endurance & the occasional sensation

of reentry into what kind of world this is.
How investors now trade water futures

& for the first time, what's human-made
outweighs what lives on this planet.

No one I know has *portfolios*,
but we hear of rising stocks

generating more wealth
for no one we know.

78% are at least somewhat concerned
about the growing level of inequality.

48% are very concerned,
the survey says, indicating all odds

in favor of a rev, & yet. The state where I live
legalized autonomous delivery robots,

classified as pedestrians. The country where I live—
its surveillance of us surveilled by the country I'm from—

has endless funds & capacity to terrorize those
without the right documents, arrest someone for making off

with baby formula. Some in my family say *There are proper
channels to citizenship*, having overridden their own

origin stories years ago. In adapting to regional customs,
one becomes a citizen of border & bootstrap mythologies.

I'm fully local-presenting now, assuring various robots
that I'm not a robot several times daily,

microdosing Adderall from a friend's Rx to achieve
a smooth email voice, obediently separating recyclables

even if I've seen it all carried off in the same truck.
Who am I to say what's sustainable

in the face of the daily death ticker.
The only economy I know is stem cuttings,

pickled cabbage, shared logins, the same $20
passed around more urgently now.

The luckiest among us score *mental health days*—
what might, in an alternate timeline,

be the ability to simply exist. *Take care*
is just a sign-off & not in the purview of policy.

As government-funded weather modification programs
make it rain by launching rockets full of silver iodide

into the clouds, it can be calming to think about
celestial objects moving around

in ancient patterns that precede all our fuckups.
That meddle with our lives in ways unknown to most.

The coming Great Conjunction is a time to release
old habits. Maybe I'll quit trying to find oblivion

in someone else, when there's a usable one
waiting among these slow days

of everything filed as pattern or scarcity.
Squirrels gorging on pumpkin innards.

Muffled name-spelling at the pharmacy counter.
Runners stretching their hamstrings on stoops.

Friends shit-talking what dead poets said in letters
after running out of current gossip.

We deride the algorithms for not getting us,
as if searching & lurking signal anything,

save for all this muted hunger. I'm no exception,
dreaming of how different my life could be

if I had a delicate neck tattoo or hex-countering
floor cleaner. My algorithm delivers

a $200 workshop on clearing ancestral traumas
& inherited unconscious impulsions,

plus a $1,240 purse made to resemble
a croissant—but I've already spent

my poetry grant on back payments
& one truly decadent burger.

It's somewhere toward the end
of the Anthropocene & still I want

to fall in love the the Wong Kar-wai way,
though I have the heart of a slacker

& everyone seems too woke or weary
for a ruinous type of intimacy.

Leaving the productivity app kills
my productivity shrub.

After so many days of blue light, I miss
creature comforts like karaoke duets

& wobbly elbow-linked walks &
buckling into someone's palm,

a real voice in my ear.
Big pink neon with its yellow spur

outside Boot & Saddle blinks off
for the last time as someone says

we'll have it all back someday.
A rowdy bacchanal awaits

those of us left, & I'd ask
who's buying if we hadn't already

watched the doomsday clock nudge
forward again. If I had flinched then.

ALIGHT

First 48 hours post-landing are
the sweet spot: part troposphere,

brain a bundle of unguarded nerves,
generous to every rush of perception.

Swayed by how locals say *That's alright*,
hand wave putting kindness back into the air

instead of *You're welcome*, as in
a transfer of something owed.

After two carafes of wine, burrow back
into someone else's word-hovel:

all hangover, all hummingbird-hearted,
a bundle of sensitivities.

But corporate's got this,
so I'm selling out.

So I'm crying in the battery-powered
candlelight of this overpriced brasserie.

One day per time zone is the accepted
recovery rate for jet lag.

Maybe this applies to other bodily phenomena
like vulnerability, wherever that gets made.

Hacking body with light could speed jet lag recovery
explains the internet.

I'm a feelings hack;
it wasn't always this way.

I used to trust them, whatever
they were in the moment, to lead.

To fall in love with anyone
all you need to do is answer
36 questions, says the *Times*.

Hey, I was wondering—

Do you have a secret
hunch about how you will die?

It took an acid trip to dredge
my first love epiphany to the surface.

Allie said, *What are you afraid of?*
while I shook in the pitch-dark woods.

Being so certain.

The Brits are indiscriminate with terms of endearment
despite their low thresholds for sentimentality.

Darling, dearie,
love, love, love.

The bus driver,
the deli cashier,
the receptionist.

I mean, yeah, it's just a word.
But when I think of your face,

the word becomes mist.
When I tell myself to think on that,

the thought ricochets
so I shut the light off.

Gala says of her girlfriend,
I summoned her, now I deal with her.

Devotion like the best curse
you can hope to suffer.

Once, we held out for months
waiting to learn who was crueler

& I wanted you to win.
The hungry ghost feigns

omnivorous, only to gorge
& spit it all back up.

Swish past cows, wildflower fields,
towns with fairy-tale names.

Businessman's intermittent throat clearing
even pleasant.

Futile spy with my black trench, flip notebook
full of obvious things:

longing, "Appleford," morning glories,
distance as a safety catch.

Want to keep riding this train into oblivion,
head suddenly absent of the usual static.

Intrusions like existential tailspins or deadlines
do exist, are presently unknown.

Warmed in my favorite scarf & thinking of
the Lewis Warsh poem I read to your voicemail

because it had the lines

Denying something, I sometimes
think, is the same as admitting
it. I admit you into my thoughts
without even trying.

& I do, & now it's time
to disembark.

Thought I'd chainsmoke around the clock here
but am never relaxed enough.

Upright in the open office, watching trees whip around
waiting for the poem to stop before I'm found out,

or wedged between two chemists
on the train, talking molecules

while I glare into the book Emma lent me:

People who are harder to love pose a challenge,
& the challenge makes them easier to love.

Slump into the seat, tune back
to the chemists & their compounds.

But the book goes on:

People who want their love easy don't really want love.

Made it this far
without mentioning the rain.

Here it is; it's perfect.

As relentless as movies & that
Magnetic Fields song have us believe.

I carry an umbrella but never use it,
head wrapped like a babushka instead.

Another way in my ever-expanding
list of ways to feel less American.

Which is to say, elegant in the face of
my boorishness.

at least my reflection
looks otherwise, I think,

then call my mother & see how long I can
go without English interludes.

I forget the word for *restless,*
though she's been saying it

my whole life long.

OUR PEOPLE DON'T BELIEVE IN TEARS

For Gala Mukomolova

I pull the Death card &you go *Know what this means?* not unkindly.
Something crucial about living keeps grazing me by inches. No grip
on my future. As we say, *nu i chto?* As we say other times, *& so what?*
Our people toast relentlessly to health, don't fall for anyone's easy grin.
We learn guarded early. In certain company, I'm cowed. I hollow out,
for ease of relations. My parents never knew Marina loved Sophia until
they heard it on the radio, decades after the poet's death. *Things were
complicated then*, they said. *You couldn't just live as yourself.* At Riis
with you, tits out & facing heavenward, I regard my debts to our legion.
In every direction: bodies gleam, however they present. To be legible
is a release. Someone's hairdye trails fuchsia wake across the water.
Someone chugs rum on the sandbar. Someone dares leather getup
in rippling heat. Everyone believes in disco. Bliss takes a day-sized bite.
We're no longer there or then, & yet: Yelena Grigoryeva will be murdered
in St. Pete tomorrow. For living as herself & loudly. Tomorrow, we will
make blini from my babushka's recipe & lament over our split culture.
Jokes cut with our first tongue, the one that tends toward withholding.
My parents never knew I loved _____. Occasionally, my mother asks
if therapy is *working*. Our people prefer their tea & humor darker.
Where were you when you first realized how many more of us exist?
I was here, waiting dimly for my undoing.

CEREUS

As loss illusion goes, you feel
more pain in losing something

than pleasure in getting it. That's how
want becomes the narrative engine,

what else? its faithful pump. You learn
to dislocate ardor & throw it into a look,

to catch your death drive gleaming
off a plane wing, awash in golden light,

to repeat *I know what I am*
when you want to wriggle out

from under any thumb—a safe phrase
too empty to question, same as

I have my reasons, as do you,
& we drape them over ourselves

all night. I'm never called *fierce*
unless it's aesthetic measure,

but I'm fixing to become a ruthless
domme of my own heart, though

it doesn't fit any disposition I've held.
If given the Marshmallow Test,

even now, I'd grope for the reward.
Hey hive mind, can you recommend

some healthy modes of debasement
in the area? When I said my sex life

was hexed, my roommate scolded
Not every day can be Cirque du Soleil, Alina.

The spirit is GGG, but the flesh
is tired of ante-upping parlor tricks,

like when a recent date
asked for electro-stimulation—

little concentrated shocks, he said,
I just wanna fuck with my dick electrified.

We've each got our ways of keeping
the lights on. When I go on my nerve

as that beloved poet prescribed,
I succumb to my porous will,

little concentrated shocks.
What one calls tenderness, the other
recognizes as swapping traumas
until someone taps out first.

What one calls *lust between us*, the other
recognizes as her default thrum.

One called our daze *sorcery*,
but naming should never precede

foreplay, or at least a finger licked
& stuck out to check for a current.

I was born into this life during
the Week of Sensitivity,

but I'm learning to become
a night-blooming cactus:

to live exactingly, with less,
to cast augury inward

to hold back until conditions are optimal
to unfurl only when I so desire.

PLACE

There's the place I'm from. Where my mama went on clandestine blue jean missions. And the place I recall. Izmaylovsky Park daffodils, dedushka still alive & just outside the frame. And the place as composite of retold anecdotes, toasts, Rusfilm hits I watch for the first time as an adult. As if to be reminded.

I love to recount how the first McDonald's workers in Moscow were trained to smile. What do I get to claim, or blame when convenient? How I flicker off so easily. What some call aloof. My penchant for benign scams & bargain scouring.

I'm from a place, I'm fond of saying, where statues of poets are ubiquitous. Where I got this love of such long walks.

On a Russian podcast, they say *sneekerhede* & *eenflooenser*. There's my sheepish indignation. There's the language a language becomes.

There's the place I return to, yet can't find. But when someone compliments my undiluted pronunciation, I'm proud. As if it means the place still exists in me, beyond making a decent salad olivier or the ushanka I pull out each winter.

You often seem somewhere else, said someone in my bed. As if to explain.

LANDSLIDE (LIVE) FT. MELBOURNE SYMPHONY ORCHESTRA

The lake is boring & we adore it—
light talk batted from your rock to mine.
In the lulls, I'm elsewhere already, wondering
how many of you there will be, how many lakes,
how many shimmery days like this.
Iannone told an interviewer, *When I was young,*
I wanted Eros to be durable. Mine feels
expressly built for transport, tucked
within this youth (my flickering pilot light)

For at least a few more years, someone will
arrive & fit into the scene easily as you do now,
placated & squinting just this way. The refractory period
is no time for gravitas, but I want to know
what it means to embarrass oneself for love
& get a little sadder, thinking now
of no one I miss.

SPIT

Her profile reads *In town for the weekend, trying to feel something—*
a challenge or a plea, contingent on the interlocutor. Asking anyone
to make you feel is one way out, but the execution is a mixed bag.
Where does anyone empty their want of its brutal clarity?
Week 3 of government shutdown: visitors off-road at Joshua Tree,
carve new desire paths in the absence of rangers.
The FDA quit inspecting food, so we may as well fill our mouths
however we like. Empty our fantasies into whatever expanse is left.
Big sky & all that. Another's spit. Conrad advises rose quartz
in my water bottle. I smoke a rose quartz pipe instead, shotgun
softness back in. Desire meaning longing fouled. Permeable memory.
A sacred wedge between ourselves & industry. Has me one minute
histrionic & dire as a stormcloud bursting. The next, screenshotting
affirmations in the backseat of a stranger's car. A long lineage of women
who prefer to be left alone with their thoughts inhabit my blood.
What's hot one night disorients now. But we'll try it again & again.

TOSKA

Days a cascade of what.
Trolley clatters thru a grimy warmth.

Hours filled with what.
Dimming light as stabilizer.

What you call me in the dark
isn't what I am

& that helps me float
above the moment.

Is that what anyone
means by role play?

Men point out the moon
like we haven't been conspiring

this whole time. Like I haven't
been right here, renegotiating

the terms of my objectification.
Let me give you the highlight reel.

That's not how time works,
but still

I say *Not dtf,*
spiritually drained,

You say *That's sweet,*
thanks for sharing.

No equivalent for
toska in this tongue

so I gape & gape
at anonymous greenery

spewing from a neighbor's porch.
Birds flicker in & out of view

with nothing to tell. I can't
write what I can't identify.

What happens when
you want to assign meaning

for protection, absolution,
to move past the incident,

reclaim your body after
the incident, quit calling it

the incident, hitch on to a word
& use the word as foothold—

In school, my mother learned
all the names of mushrooms

from primeval forests far out
past the city & the dachas.

Cautionary tales about crones
& hungry wolves & wicked hearts

lost, like so much else, in the gap
between the old world & this

amerikanka, launching immigrant
daughter guilt into the receiver

while my mother gains traction
in the hatched narrative that she'll die

before her firstborn's settled. If
there's a love without encumbrance,

I don't need to know it. At my age,
she had two kids & three jobs.

At my age, I have a busted phone
full of contacts filed under *That was*

a weird period in my life, actually
Awe is rare & sometimes grotesque

& it's not that I don't know
what I want;

I just don't know how to
want the same things

for a long time
& what I don't want

can happen anyway, has happened,
moves trackless, finds me slouching

thru an esoteric French film
about complicated love. You know

the kind: all the players deranged
& beautiful, ready to bleed out

for it. The woman in purple eyeshadow
screams *I love you means nothing.*

Later, someone offers *Sorry*
I was disappointing tonight

in response to my body coiled
around itself.

Stay if you want
means nothing beyond reflex—

proof I've been socialized
to show contempt benignly.

I'm alright—leave the air
stilled after a sudden storm.

MEANWHILE

I'll never know the name for what I wanted
when I slid downhill in the snow & made no motion to brake or divert,
pitched into a tree, staggered upright, waved okayness
Easy to say something about knowing one's limits, & I do:
manageable hazards with explicit outcomes.
Easier to say I wasn't paying attention than explain trying to relocate
the brute immersion I've chased my whole remembered life—
buzzy jolt, ear-ringing after impact.
What happened in the pit at shows & now mostly
in acts I describe from a distance. If only because there's no word
for wincing in gratitude. Or freezing up, mid–tightrope walk
between ardor & escapism.

There's power in specificity: the more exact our phrasing,
the more precisely we experience the world. The better
we can make out what's missing. I mistook blank space for boundlessness.
The looks we exchanged for perception. Flushed, mid-fuck faces in the mirror
for a sort of glory. Blunt force for being altered. Standard-issue potentiality
for something headier. *So many of the words are for meanwhile,* Jack Gilbert wrote,
& meanwhile's a way of being placated. As in adjacent to. When it happens,
the white light I wager my body for passes as transcendence,
if only for an instant.

BLOOD MOON

You have a new memory.

The Cloud in my hand swells
with burnished Southwest sunlight.

My avatar shown relaxed, not tugging
the laundry line of her wants.

August is an inconsolable month
spent gulping lushness at the edge
of the treeline. After the mystic warns
to be careful around low-vibration people,
I ask around to see if anyone wants
to switch appetites for a week
so I can understand moderation.

This reality is so fixed & it can't always
be a matter of escaping to other realms, right.

Molly says that when she can't sleep,
she imagines each of her friends' hands.

My date says *I hope it wasn't anything I did,*
38 min after I arrive.

Raena says, *I'm wearing a bodysuit,*
come get me, just in time.

Tsvetaeva says, *However much you feed a wolf,*
it always looks to the forest.

Jayson says, *Stay grounded, love*
after we get high for four days & four nights
in a protective measure against the blood moon.

We dip our fingers into a black bowl
& light dollar-store candles, listening to Toni Braxton.

Intentions are what matter here.

Lifestyle choice is a term above my paygrade.
This is how my life came to me, askew
& baring its unsatiety, beckoning toward
the next astonishment.
Sometimes it's hoodoos with bands
of white & rust-orange
or rustle of tumbleweed,
dust whirl, dim lavender skyscape.
Sometimes it's a you-abstraction.
Mostly it's my friends, their hearts crystal-bright
& down to be slung wherever this summer.

We're losing a minute of light each day now,
hurtling toward the solstice.
There's a gentle resignation in Cohen's voice
when he sings, *Ah but you got away,*
didn't you babe, like the turning of lovers
isn't our business to think through
beyond its experiential truth.

I masturbate before walking to the co-op
to feel more certain about my guac selection
& the long, lone shadow
I accompany home.

I ask my phone:

What time is sunset

What kind of moon tonight

What song was playing when my heart's chambers
got thrown open to let these breezes in?

SUPPLICATION

I want it this way:
pheromones tripping or otherwise fixed.

See: the teeth incision tattoos
a love three springs removed & I commissioned
as a reminder of the deranged state
we stayed in only long enough
to commemorate, & just as well.

Or else: wall-gazing while shadows move
across an apartment with slick floors for spinning,
a fire escape with its marquee of leaves,
& a bed always unmade as if to say
the days never break quite so cleanly.

Some remarkable disruption could arrive
in the middle of things, or even now
carried along the breath—

HARD PEOPLE

Watching old Soviet animations as a sort of secondhand nostalgia, our languages meld into a makeshift one. With cartoonish accent. Not the one our parents have, which we can't actually imitate, or the one we shift into when we get drink-slurry or pissed off. Closer to the one we hear people put on & immediately know they aren't one of us.

Someone on a forum asks, "Why are Russians such 'hard' people?"

One response: *When you have to do with almost no resources for generations you [sic], develop mentality of philosophers. When you are trained for generations that nothing is yours, you don't mind to share, it's better then [sic] being made to give it. Sometimes with fingers still attached.*

You tell me how your father, a professor in Moscow, slept in parks & train stations, having been denied housing. I tell you how my dedushka, a self-taught master tailor, refused to work for the Bolshoi unless he could hire other Jews. *A real mensch*, the rabbi said at his funeral. In those years, I was told, anyone looking for a synagogue knew to ask for directions to a particular theater with a rotating code name.

Knocking on wood isn't enough to cast off generational trauma, so we were taught to do it thrice. Then spit over the left shoulder, the devil's side. When I was very small, they tried getting me to write in Cyrillic with my right hand, but it didn't take.

Our names are the ones our families changed them to be when we arrived. And what are we? I'm a Hebrew-school dropout. At your bat mitzvah, the Torah reading was transliterated into English. We call ourselves *culturally Jewish*. Ruskis with an asterisk. Still, in our mother tongue, we say наши—*ours*—to indicate *one of us*.

DURA

When the universe winks,
I wink back reflexively.

As now, "Part-Time Lover"
on the taxi radio & my head

half out the window
grinning at bleached sky

on waterway, this life caught
in a protracted moment of buffering.

The song's talk of illicitness
& discretion rings quaint:

an affair, in its exactitude, marks
the lover as wrong, full stop.

A useless gauge if the stakes
aren't so linear, as here.

In durak, the player left holding
cards is deemed the fool.

There's no option to fold
if you foresee it—

wait for defeat or play like
you don't know it's coming.

I haven't decided to leave you yet,
but I can envision it today

in this pocket of bliss, my body
hazed with your brackish stink.

Last week, I tried to lose a man
at the gallery, but he kept

appearing, palm on my back,
to ask what I thought. I thought

only of a lost capacity to ignore
discord for carnality's sake.

Dura, dura, sang Vadim
when I lost. The table laughed

& so did I. That's how it goes:
I don't know I'm a dura until

the universe winks & I squint
to determine whether

it's an illusion. As if knowing
alters the outcome.

THIS DAY IS A WASH

for Rachel Milligan

when   I'm too candid for abstractions
        absence isn't lack, but inadequacy thrown into relief
        it's my turn to say, *I'm not comfortable with the arrangement*
        morning is a hook piercing the jowls
        delays between our answers lengthen

when   I keep a lavish sample spritzer for when & only when
        the when is catatonic at the clinic for I lost track of how long,
        but at least I smelled elegant
        the rain turns torrential, as if cued
        the magic 8 ball gets stuck edges-up, rejecting its own limited outcomes
        wonder is coming back for us, but not yet
        you try to leave your body, but the severance doesn't take

when   the news dares us to stay brave
        the news gives us the spins
        the news becomes vomit in a pristine hotel toilet
        this is no time for grace
        I cave first & call from the stairwell, where things are allowed to get personal

when   I petitioned the patron saint of all things prurient, I forgot to be specific
        the city shrinks to fit my palm
        I leave, the sun will be wedged between treetops
        we *live & breathe our customer-focused culture*
        I log my absence in the absence management program

when   our bodies carry on with secret dealings during sleep
        you look at me just so & I go *what?* to diminish it
        friends kiss on the sidewalk wearing uncertain spring haircuts
        aberrant weather lets us feel okay longer, though not without guilt
        memory clamps around what all wasn't meant to happen

when   her voice trails affection around the bedroom
       someone says, *This is going to get weird*, there's a sure sign it won't
       checking whether I've forgotten already means I haven't
       lovers along the tolerability continuum are known as *situations*
       you snore within minutes after finishing, I hallucinate concepts like *husband*

when   I gained agency because I learned how to aim
       a fist uncurls inside my throat & I'm rapturous, emptied of all objectives
       I mean shock to the system, the overtone is sex
       our proclivities meet in a subhuman state, that's called a miracle
       a siren call needs retuning, where do you take it?

when   I understood how a touch can be both game & wholly indifferent
       my body is returned in working order, it's both comfort & disappointment
       every welt, every shudder, every shower-whistle is a well-worn route
       you about-face at the corner, but my pulse holds steady
       the rousing spell has run its course—

COMPOSURE

Of course,
you can go days
without a revelation
or even an idea.
The draft stays unsent:
Sorry, babe,
been out of sorts.

What's that French phrase
meaning 'sweet note'
& did millennials kill it
along with Applebee's,
napkins, homeownership,
fabric softener, savings,
& putrid, distinctly
American idealism—
I mean, finally.

Now we walk under
a wide, blue yawn
not talking much,
fascinated by apples
as we yank them
off branches,
a perfect leaf
stuck on one
& I show you
proudly, as if
I made it.

A day I'll keep
filed under *idyllic*
long after the relations
enter syndication
or transpose
onto someone else.

My memory
does this when low
on bandwidth,
grafting faces & years
& cities onto each other.
At a panel on Larry Levis,
someone spoke admiringly
of his prolific hoeing
& I think, not a bad legacy.

Today has a waterfall
in the distance, sparkling
trick of the light
like the *Étant donnés,*
foil cascade over
an electric motor
turning inside a tin
& what was the nude?
his wife's hair,
his lover's curves
or maybe
the other way around.

One of your lovers on the porch
another across from me
& one of hers

at the head of the table
everyone smoking
something, hard
at work determining
what prospective
couplings are left
& I'm tuned
into the cicadas,
wanting to join
but what part of the body
makes a sound so primordial.
What part regulates composure
& where's the switch?

You fuck my thoughts
into an alluring static
& I drive head-on
into the mist, warbling along
to a sad song
stuck between frequencies,
honeycrisp clenched in my
teeth like a weapon.
Three hours later, I pick up
Danielle, who says,
You're a strong queer woman
& you will not miss this turn

By now you know
it's early autumn
& the moon's a druzy,
I call this my power season,
which means
I say *More*

& then I say *More*
& eventually come into
what I can't withstand
or otherwise
I straighten up
& plant my flag.

AURA

Steep in euphoric recall by dragging the same thought
from one end of the mind to the other—

a muffled song skipping until it comes through distinctly.
Where does it all go? Time, I mean,

if you only need to cover idling, art, overlapping perversions,
an occasional decadent breakfast.

I don't believe in the grind, or where it ever got anyone.
For years, I've directed my laptop to install the critical update tomorrow,

& it goes on like this. By one partner's count, it's our sixth season
of feelings-adjacency, & this too goes on:

tier of knowing in which you reach a silent mode of drift compatibility.
Post-limerence, *come by* means mostly sleep, hold each other

through heavy shit. Chronos churns on, but kairos you've got to chase
soon as you catch sight—lap it up like ice-cream drip

on a wrist, arm outstretched into a West Philly sunbeam.
The truth is, some things are so totally fine,

like pride in keeping several small- to medium-sized plants,
some pets, & each other alive, day after day,

into this one, with its sudden uptick in tulips
& the early evening's balmy sheen.

My aura's leaking in the streets, I mutter to Jennie
after the stronger edibles kick in. It's fine,

it's still fine—& we link arms, let ourselves
believe in the endeavor Stanford called

magic against death. We let the strangeness
course through us, take the long way out.

RE: EROS

Do I look alive enough out here?

Crushed velvet signaling my intent to be devoured, undone, et cetera,
whatever else shows veritable effort. I want useless splendor, to be as carried off
with rapture as the woman who kissed a Twombly hanging in a gallery, later said

It was a gesture of love . . . I did not think it out carefully.
I want the class wars to start, but everyone's so tired. All these neologisms
for disruption & innovation & still, not a soul I know confuses precarity with play.

Eros, I've looked for you all over. Our totalitarian state glitched out my libido
& I give over whole afternoons to huffing lavender, hitting up ghoulish senators,
browser history littered with herbal elixirs & all the things I should know

how to do by now. All around me, women grip the buoys of their autonomy
to stay afloat until personhood washes up on the shores of no nation.
I stockpile intimacies almost too ephemeral to clock:

strangers act so kind whenever I wear this ridiculous pom-pom hat,
& old friends use my name's diminutive, & some lovers leave
a glass of lemon water by the bed, my body carved with red filigree.

Desire doesn't aspire to anything other than itself—
I don't miss so-&-so, just being seen in that way. Just having
an unholy place to rest, set all this down.

ELUSIVE BLACK HOLE PAIR

Such a time to be alive!

What comes after
the ever-accelerating failure
of the American experiment hangs
in the arid horizon beyond you
snipping basil with beatific focus

Whenever I say
Let's, you say *When*?

I mean it,
this thing about

the urge to go on
Your kinetic way is only to blame

I'm no longer terrified of vastness

My love

Let's abscond

Find some galaxy

some town

some meadow

in which to become

stranger & stranger

SACRED BATH BOMB

So come my friends, be not afraid / We are so lightly here
Leonard Cohen

We can't take any of it
with us to the other side of the veil
So what's it matter if the huge soaking tub
is mine or a moneyed stranger's?
Repeat that to a mind unable to tune out
how unhurried bliss & love minus
the pallor of scarcity are most attainable
for those who score shout-outs in hefty wills,
while some slice off a little Good Life
through grift or proxy, & others get legit
distracted by the concept of striving—
or as Jack just texted, *We are but specks*
in space & this is what you choose???

Here's to the rest of us, fixated on cosmic dealings
ancient beyond human intervention.
Give us our daily digest of microplastics
& plots to place ads in our dreams.
Anonymous donors sponsored today's witnessing
of Art & I treated myself to a bath bomb
while reading about the demise of the Choco Taco
& why "no one" "wants" "to work" "anymore"

Among the many natural predators of poets,
mine include developers, executives, khaki-wearers,
talking appliances, & the people who respond,
every job I've had since adolescence.
I'm still holding out for dream gigs like UFO hotline operator

& the hot-dog barge guy high-fiving sun drunks
noon 'til dusk on the Delaware River,
or anything that involves choosing what happens
with one's day for more of a day than not

Conditions are ripe for a new mystic, but all that
fervor & discipline goes against my divine purpose
of hanging out, noting as many good uses for
my body before I've got to leave it behind.
The latest when Warren & I kicked off our shoes
to dance with the Sun Ra Arkestra on cemetery grounds
The atrium shot through with sweat-and-sequin glow
& sounds of assurance that the astral realm is real,
unlike the alienating notion of Tuesday, 6:37 pm

More citations needed re: that Norwegian island
voting to abolish time, & W. S. Merwin not picking up
his phone for 30 years in service of the Muse
I'm not even trying to get off the hedonic treadmill—
only to figure out how others manage to slow it
Where a revelation would be, the poem
gets lukewarm tub water with a violet fizz
of glitter—its indestructible glint
as good as stardust in some distant karmic cycle

SATURN RETURN

Everyone hurries a touch in the moody weather
while others consider what it means

to feel calmer in risk's orbit, ruthlessly
down for whatever. Even or especially

if it stings. Good morning, universe,
with your sudden biting air—

My erotic imagination remains on sabbatical
despite many blessings in the house of novel apparatus

& the alleged libido spike tied to this astrological transit
as consolation for its relentless cataclysms.

I tried to look moved when you showed me
a vibrator that doubles as an alarm clock

though most days, I wake trembling around
the edges & think, *What rot awaits?*

which cancels out both my OPTIMUM CHILL banner
& the cleansing effects of a salt lamp

my mother gave me because she suspects
I'll never want to have children.

This may be true, since our economic system
is structurally rigged to swindle the working class—

but for this, my murky chakras
aren't to blame.

Based on break-room discourse,
the approaching cuffing season

isn't nearly as kinky as it sounds,
& hinges on a crude sense of exigency.

Back in my reality, some friends
avoid saying *partner*

as it indicates a hierarchy
& this harshes the egalitarian vibe.

Power dynamics maintain
their hobbyist appeal, while the riddle

of merging my life's infrastructure with another's
sublimates me into a gentler form.

To demonstrate why this is important,
I gesture now at the unstable world.

More than 100,000 want to go to Mars
& not return, reads the headline.

I'll wait right here & bore a path
into the center of the earth using just my anxiety,

or carry out the neoliberal conspiracy
of self-care: *Rumours* on repeat

& a man-repellant shade of lipstick
named *dirty money*—smudge-proof

for all those late-late capitalist nights
spent tidying this condition to let someone in.

After returning from a wedding, I dart
around him for days, just in case

nesting is a communicable state
or desire molds to its closest container.

When he sends a fresh batch
of dick pics, my equilibrium returns

in the stillness
of remembering

we're merely dopamine vampires
trying to skirt the mortal coil.

Bleak humor suits
my Soviet blood

& everything does feel fine
when Rachel says,

Do you know anybody
who is okay right now

with the question mark
deliberately left out.

Reclaiming my life
meant divesting

explains an article about hoarding.
As if I get to choose how long

her muted perfume clings, or apply
logic like a compress to the forehead.

The difficulty of divesting isn't
in the discarding—

it's in knowing what to keep.
But I recall our particulars all wrong,

which is to say incandescently.
Which is to say I romanticize

the lack of understanding that keeps
predictability or comfort

from permeating *our thing.*
Nothing's nailed down

in this holding pattern
of torpor & grope.

Limp parts left out in case of mood lifts.
Drape swell & recede.

Hoarse mouth suctioned to a shoulder.
Language held taut.

& my oracular heart resigned
to hit snooze again.

So much for your fixed sign.
A wobbled laugh on delay.

ROUTE 1

When you ask what I'd do if I woke up tomorrow & didn't have to worry over money, I tell you the truth. Commission a clamshell-shaped bed that snaps shuts on command, then close out my filial piety—tickets to St. Pete for mama, a team of attentive doctors for papa—& the tab where I searched, *What happens when die with debt.* You smile, tactfully pull out your wallet again.

I wake early to move $$$ between accounts, take dull pleasure in washing the rental's uncorroded cookware, wonder how much the bedsheets cost. The vista of burnt fields just past the vineyard, duck liver, absurdly soft paper towels in the bathroom all say *class traitor*, though I'm only a visitor.

But cold sea spittle in my gullet is free. So's scrambling up the cliff's ferny sides, letting a gentleness permeate my thoughts. At the verge of the greenest it gets, I try to resist peering over. To stay where it's vertiginous. Like Ana wrote, *Let us surround ourselves with / Stupid pleasures.* Pockets full of clacking beach stones & no reception for hundreds of miles. Fat dragonflies & orange, reddish, maroon starfish. Card games on an overturned barrel in a seaside dive bar's backyard. The orchestral arrangements of frogs. Purple claws of echium, salt-rubbed slatted houses, downy roadside apricots. How we smell alike after days on the road. Are covered in each other's hair.

These sinewy manzanitas were once ocean, a placard mentions. Every millennium, a new terrace of land added. I'm inordinately obsessed with time lapse, given how little sense I have of it. And sex, given how often it doesn't match what's in my head. Perhaps because of that.

I consider writing about the threesome that never happened after the dive, as if it did. Some fantasy to pull from. Rather than drifting off with one arm draped over him, a leg draped over the other him. *Law & Order: SVU* in the background. But the actual wins out, in all its inelegance. Laughing at the breakfast counter next morning, passing ketchup & ibuprofen.

A hand on my knee while curving around a coastal highway begs the question: what sort of sickos invented offices & economies? And don't we think the UFOs came around already, felt the vibe, & got too disgusted to bother? Thousands of miles away, someone's huffing my dirty laundry & telling me so. The sun's cast works toward golden at a Californian dally. And I linger along.

NOW THAT I AM IN REYKJAVIK & CAN THINK

After the ring road followed wide & serpentine for hours
& now in a lava field, watching Joe & Ryan pick crowberries

for jam, chattering in the secret dialect a couple takes on
after a certain number of years, I think of you

or rather, *The Ethical Slut*, 2nd edition, Chapter 7: "Abundance,"
wherein the authors lay out their argument

against a starvation-economy approach to love,
how it's not this finite resource, so shake off your cultural programming

& desire to possess—instead, get better at scheduling,
an art I can't execute with finesse, & that's partly why

I'm here without you or any of the others,
though one of your curls held fast this whole way,

lifted off & landed here in the cushioned moss, which grows so slowly
with an idea of order I totally admire but cannot fathom.

Here as home as anywhere, I'm a Laelaps in runny nylons
roaming from mouth to mouth, secrets left intact

in the babble before I return to mortal with wholesome hemline,
then the harbor to gape dumb at the midnight sunset

& wonder if one can bore into another with such precision
that the hunger is perfect & all you sense, even in summer,

these long stretches with no darkness as a comfort to settle you,
so every big idea dilutes into a buoyant postcard signed *Yours*

Sending love from this smoky cove
flush with episodic arguments in favor of constant motion,

each gorgeous detail the only of its kind
& the mind's dazed shutter relentless to capture

this sublimity, this proof we should be tender,
given our undoing drifts in just the same.
As muscle memory is made stubborn,
so it can reprogram: like the trick where

I pinch longing mid-shudder, save it for another
time. Get the shower good & scalding,

head out divine & untethered
into the endless day.

VULNERABILITY ENGINE

Fuzzy sunlight,
lines coming in all clipped.

I cast off gaggy assurances on tea bags,
chocolate foil, the yogurt lid, etc.

My form is a body—got it.
I even know some of its constraints:

can't open intimacy like a door,
sighs to propel itself around,

starts to visibly emote & backpedals
into *Hard to explain over text.*

There's a sort of stamina
in hanging out, waiting

to feel certain, or to arrive—
how limited your motions become.

Emma writes, *I just want to hop
from dysfunction to dysfunction*

& I think of water lilies, how each piece
of a rhizome can spurt a whole new plant.

How each new ache takes root
in adjacency to another one.

I take endless pics of my legs, framed
in a rotating series of sidewalk mirrors

while waiting to get buzzed in upstairs.
The shop owner leaves them out every day

& I've never seen so much as a crack on one.
It's the best spring my legs ever had,

pumping up & down the stairs to someone
waiting in their 4th-floor walk-up,

fucking away my lunch break, transitory banter,
tending to dailiness. I broke up with everyone

in the same dizzy spell of a week.
It was hardest with you—

I talked about liminality
& felt so foolish.

In Russian culture, to speak or
touch or hand objects over a threshold

is to invite rotten luck.
That's all I wanted to relay.

I've grown into knowing
no one registers

the gooey human displays
one self-admonishes over,

but nonetheless waited
to sob in the Twombly room—

subsumed by those giant canvases
& piling new words, a careful & hopeless cairn.

Like, *When I said*
do whatever you want to me,

what I meant was
get me out of here.

I keep still sometimes for hours
& all the wrong details creep in:

debt down to the cent, cherished faces
of those long or recently gone,

what my body withstood
felt again as a literal muscle memory.

My mother tells me how her friend Tanya
manifested her dream lover:

she bought a pair of slippers
in the dream lover's presumed size

& wore them around
while talking to them.

This helped her get a clear sense
of the dream lover's attributes,

my mother explained—
even the make & model of his car.

When Tanya's dream lover appeared,
they moved to Switzerland

with his sports car & the slippers.
It happened just that way.

If things turned out differently,
it would've been a bleak story:

a lonely woman talking to a pair
of slippers, not even in her size.

Where I come from, prosperity
& desire fulfillment hinge

on superstition & the stars,
but it's uncouth to call it out like that.

If it had turned out differently,
my mother said,

I wouldnt've told you the story—
будь проще

meaning, *Be simpler*
Or, to translate another way:

name your need,
then call it home.

I FORGET WHAT I RETURNED FOR

Wonky satellite feeling
after a birthday

as if hours will find
a suddenly altered sequence

beyond *Where to, again*

An airport vegetable aura about me—
rucked almost-freshness
easily overlooked
by someone distracted
or making do,
& they are
I mean, we

I keep idly smearing
an orange-ginger lip balm
you left in an old winter coat—
formerly loose button gone,
another newly dangling
A wisdom of our age mandates
Toss what doesn't spark joy

but I'm into bittersweet reverbs:

how objects, like nicknames,
stick around long after their sources
how people don't vanish
when you stop loving them

IMPERVIOUS THIRD

On the more explicit app, *flexible* couples seek
a *playful & adventurous third ;)*

In a long-enough lull, a slanted logic
starts to resurface:

Rapport is nearly chemistry!

Typecast is close to a type!

Fringe normativity isn't always predictable!

So on, before I recall the elusive to-dos:

Hold fast to radiance.

Enough with the bit parts.

Get in way over your head.

Shrugs are hardly anyone's erotics.
It's just, the signal cuts out when I shift

from pleasure vessel to bait, flint,
curio, companion animal, other.

When an end to longing is sensed,
what becomes of want's largesse?

As a kid, I bit the insides of my cheeks
until the cartilage toughened,

or got on a bike & came back bloodied,
asphalt-flecked. Having punctured

the membrane between self & out-there.
Having dinged up my subjectivity good.

I grew into diversions. Went farther afield.
Wore shock absorbers nearly to the bone. & sometimes,

I nearly made out the gossamer link
from heart to cunt to sanctum.

In the data dump of past encounters,
thousands come up with a commonality:

a body's semaphore motioning toward obliteration,
or at least a well-appointed waiting room.

HORSESHOE CRAB ORGY

The ecologist uses words like
prehistoric, instinctual.

It happens each spring
at high tide, moonglow.

Because there are more crabs
than viable pairings,

attachments form with clumsy
urgency. Here we laugh

at their scrambling, their
inelegant shows of need—

but how the crabs lock together
makes it harder to right themselves

in the rough surf,
the ecologist explains.

If they weren't entangled,
there's a good chance

they'd flip upright
& be okay, set back adrift.
Because he's hanging in there

The likelihood of that happening becomes more remote

But he'll die with her

DAYLIGHT SAVING

This summer in Philly, a directive to kill spotted lanternflies
formed citywide camaraderie: an outlet for our dislocated furies.

Neighbors swatted together in the swelter. Some strung
the insects onto earrings. Nothing is free in America—

that's every first gen's starting inheritance—but most anything
can become commerce. As it stands, most of waking life is spent working

so we self-style into sentience-adjacency, plus kitschy phrasing
like *Sunday scaries* & *happy hour.*

The inscrutability of my wanting makes an ever-shifting target.
Was pleasure always so conditional? Or is too much else ruptured—

& not in the quick-fix way, where a few hours of airplane mode
recalibrate the senses. Desire is propulsive, until I skid.

I wonder if anyone else can see my affections ricochet around,
in search of a solid landing. If the muses get worn out, too, & take breathers

while the golden hour's light remakes the world into a creamy
cosmic latte—the official average color of the galaxy.

When the clocks recede, I think of the boss who, when meetings
ended early, would say *I'm giving you back a half hour*, or whatever it was,

in full salute of chartering another's time. I built a paltry arsenal
of long strolls, uppers, benzos, valerian anything, Post-it piles,

a blur of someones in expensed hotel beds,
propped on elbows asking *What is it that you do, again?*

Bang to be let back into my own thoughts . . .
Consider health-care coverage a windfall . . .

Mourn the fallen moon tree (though it was a copy of another moon tree) . . .

Mourn the redwoods, fireflies, platypuses, permafrost, all else that deserves to outlive us & won't . . .

Mental math on what I can afford to enjoy . . .

Daydream what mutual care could do . . .

Daydream of everyone walking out & getting what they want & not coming back, even then . . .

Especially then . . .

Reply & reply . . . Attach the attachments . . .

The maple leaves wobble down each day, clump onto windshields.
One hitches a ride on my shoulder all the way from downtown to West

& the blinking reindeer wedged among six-pack holders in the bodega window
for years now are the only seasonal décor I abide, & oh—it's no longer a surprise

to have our sense of temporality totally fucked with.

Mid-workday, I pantomime being inconsolably turned on until we both are for real,
& I catch you grinning on-screen.

Our little grid all lit now. Time taken back, turned
into dreamy, useless goo.

I find equilibrium
in some primordial tug from the earth, urging to spin away

from the locus of enterprise, where it's painted forever evergreen
& you never learn how to keep still, each other warm.

NOTES

"Take Care" –
The survey stats are from CivicScience data published in December 2020.

A "great conjunction" refers to when Jupiter & Saturn appear closest together in the sky. This conjunction is seen as a time of ideological resets, societal change, & political upheaval. In December 2020, these planets were the closest they had been in 800 years.

"Alight" –
Psychologists have tried—&, allegedly, succeeded in — making strangers fall in love. A 2015 essay by Mandy Len Catron, "To Fall in Love With Anyone, Do This," references a 1997 study led by psychologist Arthur Aron that aimed to accelerate intimacy between two strangers by having them ask each other a set of 36 specific questions, one of which is quoted here.

The Lewis Warsh poem quoted here is "Latimer Street."

The book quoted here is Rachel Kushner's *The Flamethrowers*.

"Our People Don't Believe in Tears" –
The Marina and Sophia referenced in this poem are poets Marina Tsvetaeva and Sophia Parnok.

Yelena "Lena" Grigoryeva was a human rights and queer rights activist who was killed in St. Petersburg, Russia, in July 2019. Police obtained a confession from a suspect, but this is widely believed to have been a contract killing. Grigoryeva was an ardent critic of Vladimir Putin's regime.

"Cereus" –
The Stanford marshmallow test was a 1972 study on self-control led by psychologist Walter Mischel. Children were given the choice of waiting to receive two

marshmallows, or to receiving one marshmallow immediately. The experiment aimed to measure how well participants could delay instant gratification to receive greater rewards in the future.

The Week of Sensitivity, which falls during the Aquarius-Pisces cusp, is described in Gary Goldschneider and Joost Elffer's *The Secret Language of Relationships*, which divides the year into 48 "weeks" and includes an assessment of personality traits for each period.

"When I go on my nerve / as that beloved poet prescribed" refers to Frank O'Hara's cheeky "Personism: A Manifesto," in which he wrote, "You just go on your nerve."

"Landslide (Live) ft. Melbourne Symphony Orchestra" –
This poem's title references a recording of Stevie Nicks performing "Landslide" that I played on obsessive loop while writing this poem. You can find it on YouTube.

The quote from artist Dorothy Iannone, "When I was young I wanted Eros to be durable," comes from a November 2009 interview in *Frieze*.

"Re: Eros" –
In 2007, a woman named Rindy Sam kissed an all-white panel in Cy Twombly's Phaedrus, a triptych displayed in the Museum of Contemporary Art in Avignon, France. The quoted lines are from Sam's statements in court.

"Elusive Black Hole Pair" –
The title of this poem comes from a 2021 article by Tereza Pultarova published on Space.com. The subhead read: "Scientists expected that an elusive black hole pair might be hiding in a nearby galaxy, now they can finally see it."

"Sacred Bath Bomb"
The epigraph of this poem comes from Leonard Cohen's song "Boogie Street."

The line about natural predators of poets is inspired by C. D. Wright's "A Plague of Poets," in which she writes "Even if, as it is often said, there are too many of us—poets, that is—that the field is too crowded (as opposed to too many hedge-fund managers or too many pharmaceutical lobbyists or too many fundamentalists), time, rejection, discouragement, and the inevitable practicalities and detours (some of them fortuitous), as well as wasted energy, the slow seepage or sudden shift of interest, premature death, burdensome debt or better offers, usually cure the problem of overpopulation. In other words, there are plenty of natural predators."

"Meanwhile" –
The Jack Gilbert poem quoted here is "The Butternut Tree at Fort Juniper."

"Blood Moon" –
"However much you feed a wolf, it always looks to the forest" is from Marina Tsvetaeva's *Art in the Light of Conscience.*

"Ah, but you got away, didn't you babe" is from the Leonard Cohen song "Chelsea Hotel #2."

"Dura" –
Durak is a popular Russian card game that takes its name from the Russian word for 'fool.' A dura is the female version of a durak.

"Aura" –
The Frank Stanford poem quoted here is "The Battlefield Where the Moon Says I Love You."

"Route 1" –
"Let us surround ourselves with / Stupid pleasures" is from Ana Božičević's poem "Con Mucho Amino" in *Joy of Missing Out,* which everyone should own.

"Now That I Am in Reykjavik & Can Think" –
This poem is titled after Frank O'Hara's poem, "Now That I Am in Madrid and Can Think."

Laelaps was a mythological Greek dog that was destined to always catch its prey.

"Daylight Saving" –
Cosmic latte is the "average" color of the universe, found by a team of astronomers at Johns Hopkins University in 2002.

ACKNOWLEDGMENTS

Versions of "Alight," "Now That I Am in Reykjavik & Can Think," & "Saturn Return" first appeared in *What Urge Will Save Us,* a chapbook published by Spooky Girlfriend Press in 2017.

Many thanks to the editors of *The American Poetry Review*, *blush*, *Cosmonauts Avenue*, *Dusie*, *Elderly*, *Hot Pink Mag*, *Jewish Currents*, *Peach Mag*, *Prolit*, *the tiny*, *Thrush*, *swamp pink*, and *Wax Nine*, for publishing poems (or iterations of poems) from this collection.

I'm super grateful to:

Sebastián Hasani Páramo, Will Evans, & the whole Deep Vellum team for your belief & support. Seb—what a sublime editorial pairing. Thank you for getting me & for nudging my work ahead with aplomb, incision, & enthusiasm.

Tyler Antoine, Cynthia Arrieu-King, Levi Bentley, Zach Blackwood, Patrick Blagrave, Dan Brady, Stephanie Cawley, Jenn DiGuglielmo, Lillian Dunn, ebs Sanders, Ryan Eckes, Boston Gordon, Thomson Guster, Patrycja Humienik, Devin Kelly, Rax King, Matt Korvette, Warren Longmire, Pattie McCarthy, Jack Sadicario, Danniel Schoonebeek, Con Sheridan, Raena Shirali, & Alex Simand. This book wouldn't exist as it does without you.

The Overflowing Poetry Workshop—Phoebe Glick, Ted Rees, Irene Silt, Susannah Simpson, Ryan Skrabalak, & Ariel Yelen—for your insights & brilliance.

The Cheb Collective, especially Ana Božičević, Julia Kolchinsky Dasbach, Ruth Madievsky, Neon Mashurov, Gala Mukomolova, Luisa Muradyan, Tanya Paperny, Sonya Vatomsky, & Karina Vahitova. с любовью и солидарностью!

All the group chats that sustain me.

The queers, poets, freaks & weirdos, burnouts, whores, punks, & fellow travelers who showed me that we can carve out slivers of the world just for us. As Diane di Prima wrote, ". . . remember / you can have what you ask for, ask for / everything" Here's to more.

My family, especially my mama.

You, reading this.

ALINA PLESKOVA is a poet, editor, and Russian immigrant turned proud Philadelphian. Her writing has been featured in *American Poetry Review*, *Thrush*, *Peach Mag*, *swamp pink*, *Jewish Currents*, and elsewhere. She coedits *bedfellows magazine* and is a Leeway Foundation Art & Change grant awardee. Her chapbook, *What Urge Will Save Us*, was published by Spooky Girlfriend Press in 2017. *Toska* is her first full-length collection. More at alinapleskova.com.

CPSIA information can be obtained
at www.ICGtesting.com
Printed in the USA
JSHW020823260423
40856JS00003B/5